FEELING GOD

NOTES + REFLECTIONS

SEARCH + CONNECT + BE

MARQUITA L. MOORE

How I Grew Today, LLC
P.O Box 646
Englewood, NJ 07631
www.howigrewtoday.com

Hardcover ISBN: 979-8-9885345-0-1
Paperback ISBN: 979-8-9885345-1-8
eBook ISBN: 979-8-9885345-2-5

Cover and interior design by Jess LaGreca, Mayfly Design

Library of Congress Catalog Number: 2023911066

First Printing: 2023
Printed in United States of America

DEDICATION

MAMA,
the first Lightworker I saw in action. You inspire
my life so much. I get it now. I get everything you
were trying to tell me and show me. This book is for
you. Thank you for walking with me, always.

RIVER,
the greatest gift God could have ever given me
to nurture was you. Created at a time when my soul
was dry, He gave me a River where I could go, see my
reflection, cleanse loneliness, and quench my thirst
for love. Your mama loves you, Man. Forever-ever.

TO THOSE ON MY PATH,
who have graciously served me light, I am grateful.

We all have direct access to God.

CONTENTS

DEAR ONE

Only now have I realized that writing this book was the modality used to redesign me. Writing about my search for connection has been my mode of transportation to feel God. And when I say *feel*, I am referring not to the physical, emotional sense of the word but to the spiritual knowing, awareness, and belief that there is more to me than my human being. This book is what was used to move me into a space where I became close and personal with my humanity, my inner self, and the flow of guidance and connection that lives deep within me, the Highest Energy of existence that I call God.

Documenting what was being revealed to me in my spirit has shown me how I hungered to live my life as my most authentic self, fully and always connected to Source. Free. The price for freedom required me to witness myself in complete honesty. This was not easy, and at times it was uncomfortable. But I wanted to live in truth, no matter the cost.

All that you read in these pages may not resonate with you, and that is ok. I get it. I understand what it feels like to question and be uncertain and doubtful. I understand what it is like not knowing whether what you feel or believe is right. My hope is that by sharing my experience, it will help to lessen some of that uncertainty for you. This book is an ode to my walk on the path to Light, a devotion to the whole of my spiritual experience, even through times of uncertainty, questioning, and being uncomfortable.

If I may speak to you in a way that is plain, like we are good friends enjoying a meal together that I prepared for you in the comfort of my kitchen . . . just begin. Just start. Open yourself to live a life where you allow your steps to lead you to love, making your desire for truth, honesty, and peace real. By the way, all these words mean love to me, and all are my constant reminders of how pervasive and important love is.

My grandmother used to break off pieces of her plants and give them out to family, neighbors, and friends. We would visit around town, and her imprint could be potted in someone's yard, kitchen window, living room, or bedside table. It was like she was giving them a piece of her. The pages of this book are my pieces of plants, taken from my own growth, to be planted in the beautiful soil of your soul.

FEELING GOOD, FEELING GOD

I had this overwhelming sense of joy and intense love that came over me out of nowhere one day. I wasn't doing anything extraordinary. It was a routine day of getting things done and running errands. I tried to trace back to see what had occurred to warrant this gift I was feeling; I wanted to know what led to the feeling so that anytime I needed some joy in my heart, I could find the thread and pull it back. But nothing stood out. Joy, love that was sudden, unexplainable, that didn't need anything to happen to spark it into being, had simply arrived. I let it unfold and opened my arms, lifted my head to receive, and allowed the feeling to rush through me without any resistance. Every part of me was present. I stayed in the feeling for about three minutes or so, silent, basking. When I finally spoke, trying to put the feeling into words, all I could utter was "So good. Love feels so good. Feeling God feels so good." —MM

THE INVITATION: HOW I GREW TODAY

About 11 years ago, I started paying closer attention to myself. I spent time devoted to being my friend, and learning how to nurture and listen to myself. In the past, I thought you weren't supposed to give yourself so much attention. I thought it was self-centered and conceited to be so focused on yourself. But 11 years ago, something in me knew that it was time for me to give myself what I had been looking for in others: attention, care, love, and time. And if that made me self-centered or conceited, then I was about to be self-centered and conceited. I was ready to give Marquita my all, even though I wasn't sure how to do that exactly. I began to chronicle my days, as a way to stay present in my life. I remember taking out a spiral notebook, and I wrote "What I Learned Today" on the top of the first page, excited about all the things that were about to fill up these blank pages. I wrote down everything—what I liked, what I didn't like, what I ate, what I saw, what I read, where I went. I felt like I was in the honeymoon phase of a relationship with myself, and I didn't want it to stop.

These moments of growth—meeting new people, discovering a new book or movie, trying a new recipe—were opening me up to experience myself in a way that was on my terms, and I needed that. As simple as this may seem, I needed simplicity to connect with myself. I started to recognize that there were opportunities big and small for growth all around, every day. "What I Learned Today" was helping me grow, so I changed the name of my notebook to "How I Grew Today."

Journaling has always been an integral part of my life, but journaling in this way helped me be present and mindful during my day.

After about a month of doing this, I could feel a change was taking place. What I thought was just an exercise to get to know myself better began to expand into something so spiritual and beyond me. I began to feel a deeper sense of knowing about myself, and I felt more grounded and rooted in who I was. So I shifted my focus from outside to inside, and I started to ask myself deeper questions like "Who are you? What do you want out of life? How are you showing up in this world? Why has it taken so long for you to take time for yourself? What's been in the way of you loving yourself deeply?" My external quest for growth turned inward, and I felt it was imperative that I keep writing down the evidence of what I was experiencing as I went deeper within. I wrote down my thoughts and notes to myself, my questions, my dreams, my prayers, my revelations, and the clarity that was unfolding and deepening. I was making room inside, so my outside world could shift too.

I'm inviting you to peer into the pages of my notebooks, a compilation, evidence, of life evolving. These truth-telling pieces are where I connected to the part of me that is unlimited, authentic, and full of love. This is where my relationship with God and myself developed, and where our oneness became apparent to me. Through these words, I got to know myself in ways I didn't know I needed. You now hold my thoughtful guidebook, which was my companion as I learned to open my heart. These Divine revelations show the trail of my search, tracing the way I walked to feel God so that I could feel good consistently. It is my road map from this leg of the journey.

I invite you to my personal pilgrimage, to my awakening to the beauty of God that lives in me and in all of us, understanding what it means to live a life connected in a world that can feel so disconnected from God's love.

How I Grew Today is my daily practice, my commitment to growing in love and living as a spiritual being—one committed to becoming everything that the Creator created me to be, releasing all that may be in the way of that, and embracing everything that supports it so that I live this life as an example of what it is to live connected to God's light in everything I do and with everyone I meet.

THIS BOOK HAS BEEN MY ASSIGNMENT. WELL, ONE OF THEM.

Lightworkers are everywhere, in every industry and in all parts of the world. They are those who live a life dedicated to transforming darkness into light, first in their own lives, and then doing their part, using their gifts, talents, and individual assignments to spread more light into the world. They do this to serve others in love through the way they have learned to love themselves. A Lightworker can be anyone—an artist, architect, farmer, stylist, masseuse, chef, teacher, doctor, Pilates instructor, philanthropist, or business executive, anyone who uses their assignment to lead the way of light into the world. They have walked or are walking their own path of living life authentically and in truth.

Writing is my assignment, one of the ways I have made available for my spiritual gifts to flow through, spread light, and serve others. I use writing to help me uncover my blind spots so I can see what needs to be converted from darkness into light within myself. Only then can I extend myself and truly serve others.

My path is not one that is original, but it is unique to me. We are all able to work for Light.

I grew up in a Christian family that went to church on Sundays, sometimes tent revivals, and Vacation Bible School in the summers. And while I am so grateful for the foundation and faith imparted, I did not believe God's light was in me. God never felt personal or accessible to me. This book is not about religion, rules, or "doing" but about being. Being a spiritual person, being a vessel for truth, being your true self, being who you were created and sent here to be.

This book is about how my desire for revelation, wisdom, understanding, and spiritual growth grew. It is the way I began to understand deeply how to be in a relationship with the Highest Power (God).

The path to being has brought me so much understanding about life and to a place where I want to be an example of God's love on Earth.

Sharing my assignment has brought a mixed bag of feelings. If someone said to me, "You are going to write a book that centers around you growing and nurturing your relationship with God," I would have said, "No way." One, who am I? I'm not qualified. Two, who am I? I'm not qualified. This was my first misunderstanding. What's so beautiful about our connection to God is that we don't have to amass all this knowledge and be perfect; we just have to open our hearts and be willing to receive and courageous enough to be malleable, and then go where we are inspired to go and do what we have been Divinely inspired to do. God is in each one of us and ready to be expressed through us. My desire alone, to be in connection and to share that connection, is qualification enough. These writings are me adding my voice to the conversation around plugging into the flow of power that runs within each of us, and awakening to God's infinite, freely given, expansive love. I'm spreading light, in a world where darkness seems to crowd out the light. We need more stories, and more conversations that encourage the growth of light in the world.

My relationship with God has evolved so much: From fear to great comfort. From doubt to deep trust. From missing the guidance to paying attention and seeing how everything around me works together. From feeling separated to understanding my interconnectedness to everyone and everything in this life.

For a long time, I put God in a box. I made Him as confined and limited as I felt in my life. As our connection grew stronger, the boxes I put us both in began to crumble. My life began to open in all areas.

I like to say that I am a student being trained in how Divine Energy (God) works in life as I travel through Earth's school. I'm just like you, curious about life, about God, and about how we fit into it all. Well, I'm assuming you are like me since this book has appeared on your path.

My goal is not to convince, disprove, or dispel beliefs. I am sharing, extending myself as an offering by opening the intimate pages of my guidebook, sharing how I constructed an altar in my heart so that God's love can be expressed through me.

I'm not an expert in spirituality or a spiritual teacher with a set spiritual curriculum. I am an expert in the way God has brought me, and I teach through the sharing of that journey.

Whatever your assignment is, allow it to be used for light. Let your gifts awaken you to all the possibilities available to you, and open a deeper connection to God, yourself, and others.

THE REAL

I think it's important to tell you that I still have days when I feel less connected than others. Times when I still allow some disturbance to momentarily unplug me from the Divine part of me, from my higher self, which is aligned with God. It happens. And until my spirit engulfs this "Earth suit," which is my body, this is what comes with living here in this world. We are met with things, both in the physical and spiritual realms, that do not encourage connection, whether you follow a spiritual path or not.

But it is our responsibility to remain connected. Let me clarify: God doesn't unplug our connection, we do. So we must begin to understand when and how we get unplugged, the things that contribute to and influence these feelings of disconnection. I appreciate these moments and see them as gifts, rather than seeing them as a failure of my task—to walk in light and live from love. These disconnected moments have become guideposts, showing me how far I have moved away from love, trust, and truth.

I welcome all parts of this divinely human journey, especially the lessons that prune whatever is in the way of me growing, healing, unfolding, and loving deeper.

LET THIS BOOK BE A COMPANION ON YOUR SEARCH

This book is divided into three phases of reflection: *Searching*, *Connecting*, and *Being*.

Searching is what I began to do when I felt there was more to my life, but I had no idea how to access it or even if I could. I was not sure what I was searching for or where to look for it, but I was open and willing to move from where I was so that I could find it, even though I was uncertain.

Connecting is when I opened my heart to myself and God so that I could receive the love, guidance, and insights that are constantly flowing toward me.

Being is my dedication to living a spiritual life, in full connection, every day of my life, and what that looks like.

Use these pages as a guide. Take part in the *Moments to Feel* and let them serve as a way for you to connect with yourself through a moment of deeper contemplation.

Let my notes, questions, thoughts, reflections, and inspirations help you navigate through and be a reminder that you aren't alone, and that this path has been walked by many. May your own prayers, affirmations, and meditations spring forward, take root, and expand you so Spirit can guide you, at the pace that is suited just for you.

My hope is that you will allow yourself to feel deeply and begin to pay close attention to your life, your world, and the many messages, signs, and wonders that present themselves every day. The presence of God is always with us.

To those of you who are walking your own path but want to turn back, keep walking. And to those who may not be walking but feel like you want to, stand boldly on the trail and allow yourselves to be changed. I hope that my invitation gives you the courage to write your own guidebooks, to trace your own trails. This book has been my encouragement, my teacher, my study guide. My hope is that what you read resonates and awakens you again and again to the love, beauty, truth, and peace that grows continuously from *Feeling God*.

BEFORE SEARCHING

It was right after my son River's 9th birthday when I knew I had to do something. I was extremely unhappy and depressed. I could feel myself pretending to be OK, and I didn't have it in me to pretend anymore, and that scared me. It wasn't the first time I heard my inner voice say: "You're not OK, something's not right." But this time felt urgent, and I didn't have it in me to push through like I normally would.

I created this fairy-tale existence, pretending I was happy and trying to live in this made-up place every day. I wanted so much not to need the story that I created to feel good or happy with life. I wanted to live from truth. And not my truth, God's truth. Truth not informed and influenced by negative experiences, limiting beliefs, problems, hurts, misunderstandings, fears, and insecurities. Truth not filtered through fear, doubt, worry or concerns about what others think. I just didn't know how I would ever live from that place. I did not think I could get out of my own way enough to let go, surrender, and trust to this extent.

Most of my life I spent feeling broken, inferior, and insecure. I didn't trust myself, and I was distrustful but heavily dependent on others. I thought everyone else knew better than me. I wasn't confident that I knew what was best for me. I was full of anxiety, doubt, worry, and fear. I carried with me a belief that I was unlovable, and because of that, I lived malnourished by a lack of self-love and an excessive, unbalanced need to please people. I was disconnected from my heart; I wouldn't touch it; I couldn't touch it; I often lied to myself about how I felt and was too afraid to show others the real me most of the time. I was good at becoming a chameleon, blending in or changing myself into who I thought everyone needed me to be or who I thought I needed to be to fit in, be seen, be accepted, and be loved. I was manipulative in a way that I did not even realize was manipulative so that I could get the things my heart needed. I remember going through a phase—it wasn't conscious, but in hindsight I see that I thought I could buy love, taking care of things for people in a disproportionate manner, hoping it would be reciprocated in kindness and acceptance. I went along with things I really didn't want to do: a YES girl—young adult—and woman. I tried to hide my wounds, and I denied my pain. And I treated others poorly because of my inability to express my own suffering. An endless cycle. I also thought I could figure my way out of all these feelings that felt toxic and heavy by changing the right set of things about myself—my hair, my weight, the city I lived in, and my profession. I thought these were the things that had to change. And if I changed these things, I would be pleasing to others, and then they would accept me, and I could finally show the parts of me that I had been hiding. I thought changing these things about myself would give me the permission I thought I needed to be the true me. I wanted others to love and accept all of me, and I wanted to love and accept all of me. I thought these changes would help make this happen.

At one point, I thought I had finally reached that place. Everything was aligned, so I thought. I was married, was happy where I lived, had my baby, and finally reached my goal weight (Ha!). I wasn't worried about money; I could buy everything I wanted, go anywhere I wanted; I had access to places and things I only dreamed of—all the criteria I thought represented a good life. Everything I counted on to make me happy was within my reach. Every box was ticked, but below the surface, I still felt my unhappiness. I thought that acquiring and achieving would free me from this cycle of joy-happiness-sadness-doubt, but it didn't. I was still suffering. I remember asking God to help me. And then the bottom fell from under me.

My marriage began to yield to the crack in its foundation. The weight I had given it to show me my value, among other things, finally wore it down. It was the first of many things that had to break in order for me to recognize my need for healing. I was unfulfilled in my career and didn't believe in myself enough to put my all into what I wanted to do. I had aches and pains coming out of nowhere; I could feel my body breaking down. I was physically, emotionally, and spiritually in critical condition. Everywhere in my life, where I gave my power, whether relational or material, places and things that I made gods over me, fell apart. My sense of self was diminished. I felt alone. I remember thinking, *Is this God helping me? Or evidence of my insignificance?*

Chasing those things that I thought would make me whole made me feel fractured and further separated me from myself. I was lost. And in this lost, restless feeling, I couldn't find comfort in distractions like shopping, a few drinks, an accomplishment, a trip to some exotic place, or a relationship.

My restlessness turned into hopelessness. The looming thought that I would always feel this way was crushing me. And now, I had another life to look after, to show up for.

I wasn't okay to just suffer and sleepwalk through my life anymore now that I had a child. I know what it's like to witness a parent suffer and act like they aren't. I know what that does emotionally to the one who bears witness to their suffering. River was witnessing me walk through life as a fraction of who

I was created to be, and the thought that I could be responsible for this pattern continuing woke me up. Little did I know that my request for help would lead me to this awareness and have me running to the front of the line to search and be fully open to God and myself.

ONE

SEARCHING

We are looking for tangible things that we believe will help us find the cause of our thirst for more in life. Things that we hope will carry dissatisfaction and the feeling that something is missing, far from our lives. Never to find us again. You want to live better and more fulfilled. You want to live in the fullness of everything you were created to be, but you can't imagine doing that from where you are now in your life. That freedom to live awakened, remembering our oneness with God and what that affords us, is available to us right now. This is what we are searching for. But how do you come to this awareness? How do you know that awakening is something you even need to do? This is what the search is. This is what the journey is about. Recognizing you have been sleeping, and waking up wanting to live fully connected to Divine Love.

Ask yourself questions to see what you believe. Realize your hurts so you can deactivate the hold they have had on your life. Spend time alone; don't be afraid to see your rough parts. You have to see them. And do not be afraid to talk to God about who you think He is so He can open your eyes of understanding and reveal Himself to you in a fresh way.

9:22am / How I grew Today

NOTES ON SEARCHING

Something more has been calling me. There is more to life than what I see.

I don't know what it is, but I know that I have heard it before. What does it want from me? What does it want me to see? Where does it want me to look this time? I stare at the sky. I look intensely at the things around me. Yes, I see the beauty in the world, but there is a whisper telling me to look deeper, beyond my natural sight. There is more that offers a key to another realm of living, available to all of us, when we search, seeking the kingdom of love that is inside. Go deeper inside, not outside. Behind the words, behind the actions of another, beyond physical appearances. See a world beyond. We all have a moment or moments in our lives that bring us to a place where we feel there must be more. Those moments open the door for us to ask the question "Is there more to life than this?" How long has God been nudging me to come and see?

There is something deep down, telling us to move closer so that it can guide us on the path, but we aren't sure what that something is. To me, that something is God.

When I was younger, we belonged to this tiny holiness church in Brewton, Alabama, where Sister Royster and her husband ministered to about 30 to 40 members. Even though I was only around 7 or 8 years old, maybe even younger, I loved the part of the service where members of the congregation got up and testified about what God had done for them. Their testimonies told their reasons for seeking God. Those who wanted to share walked up the narrow aisle between the wooden pews to the microphone. "First, I want to give honor to God"; that's how they always started. I would say it with them, under my breath, as I prepared to listen with my whole heart.

I wanted to hear the stories. I was pulled in, even at that age, to the notion of transformation.

Every testimony led with something the person was going through or had gone through. A trial or test, or a complication in life that they surrendered.

Something was used to get their attention, something served as the agent to bring them to want to open their hearts, surrender their own effort, and connect to God.

Divorce, the loss of a loved one, an illness, trauma, the breaking of a heart, or the joy of love. It doesn't always have to be traumatic; I have heard stories of people changing their lives through loving someone so deeply that their love for this person awakened their desire to live life from a place deeper than the material, the external. Love led them to search for "the more of life."

Those times of emotional, physical, mental discomfort; unexpected, uncomfortable change; or even the experience of deep love serve as a light to illuminate the path to feeling God, the path to making the connection to our higher selves so we realize that we aren't the sum of only our issues and complications. The tests and the trials that have come in all forms are used to get us on the path, and they help us move farther along on the path. The longer I travel this pathway to more, I see that my tests and issues have a purpose.

Going through my own trials and issues in life, I appreciate those testimonies even more.

WHICH WAY DO I SEARCH?

Where do I search, and how do I search? What is being asked of me?

When I think about it, there has always been something that has tried to get my attention, something that has tried to nudge me to question my life so that I could live life more intentionally: A string of not so great relationships, some health setbacks, depression, anxiety, being stuck and unmotivated, feeling like I'm just moving in a circle. A continuous loop of pain, moments of relief, pain, another season of relief, then pain again. Treading on water, afraid to plunge to the bottom to see what is really pulling me down each time. To search is to choose—to choose to go deeper, to witness life beyond external things, beyond the surface. I don't have to choose to search, but I want to. The way I search is my choice, too: through the door that leads inwardly or through the one that keeps me outside of myself. Ignore, and search outside of myself. Or stay present, turn inward, and search within. Divine Energy has patiently been trying to get my attention, sparking the place in my heart that wants to know what "more" is. I can fan the spark to catch fire if I choose.

These are our choices. I have chosen them both. I thought if I ignored the feeling that something was missing in my life, the feeling would go away. It didn't. I thought if I changed things outside of myself, that would free me. It didn't.

For a long time, I ran away from my heart instead of turning toward it, which is the turn that makes the difference. Searching within led me to connection and love. There is a Commodores' song called "Sweet Love" that I heard one day. One of the verses is about searching for love, peace, and understanding. The song tells us to seek out love with all we've got (well, that was my interpretation of it). The song inspired me. I wondered if Lionel was singing about how God calls us to search our hearts for His love. And then I thought, WOW, what we are searching for wants us too. What we are searching for wants to be found. To know that what we are searching for wants us too is beautiful. That can be hard to believe and receive when you don't feel worthy of love, but think of how affirming it is to know that love wants you too. To know that love never gives up on you and will always be there to remind you of the option, the choice to be in relationship and to be guided by love's power. Sometimes we misinterpret where we are to search. We think that the feelings we have are telling us to search for bigger, for better. To quiet those feelings, we take the route that gives us physical evidence of growth and change. Bigger cars, bigger houses, bigger careers, bigger bank accounts. Those things are fine to have, beautiful to have—we are meant to be abundant and to have our hearts' desires—but if I'm looking to these things to provide me with peace, and to feel love, those things will never fill that hunger. For a little while, yes. But that missing, empty feeling always comes back.

11:06pm / How I Grew Today

QUESTIONS AND ANSWERS

Sometimes you have to interview yourself. Pose the questions that will bring you clarity. I am giving myself room to answer honestly. This self-confession will make room.

Q: Have you always known that there was more to life?

A: I've always felt like there was something. I have always believed in God. Now, that doesn't mean I haven't questioned my beliefs at different points in my life. But I have always had a sense of something greater. I remember the first time I felt this strong connection to everything around me. Everything came into focus at one time. It wasn't overwhelming; it felt natural.

I spent a lot of time by myself when I was younger. Playing in the woods across from our property or in various nooks and window seats in our house, just daydreaming. This one particular day, I was outside making mud pies in the front yard: mud pies with cereal toppings. I was so present. That's what I would say now; I was present, in tune with what I was doing. The air smelled so sweet, felt so crisp, the dirt felt so cold on my skin. I could feel my body pressed against the ground in a way that was hard yet soft, sturdy enough to hold me up but gracious enough to allow me to sink in. I remember saying to myself, I want to feel this every time I play. The next weekend I tried to recreate the feeling. I thought that feeling came from something that I had done new or differently that day. See, this is an example of how we naturally begin to search outside ourselves. I was a kid, I knew nothing about searching inside; most of us don't know until later in life. I put on the same clothes, shoes, got the cereal from the pantry, and headed outside. This time was different—I was different. My energy was off. I don't remember exactly why, but I was feeling anxious and worried, which was normal for me during that time. I was sensitive to the financial problems my parents had, the arguing, the fights, but I still wanted to try and recreate the feeling. I needed that feeling. I thought the act of making the mud pies and being in the dirt would make me feel better that day, but it didn't because I didn't feel good on the inside. Of course, then I did not understand the relationship between my energy and the need for it to be at a higher frequency so that I can perceive God's presence, as I do now. When we are stressed, worried, anxious, or angry, it's hard to perceive love, to believe it is still there. So yes, I always thought there was more, and I felt like I would always miss out on it. As time went on, life happened, and the feeling of that day got buried. But there was another time in my late 20s, where I experienced something similar, when I was present and once again everything came into focus at one time, but it was short-lived. I was still too distracted.

IN THE ALONE TIME

There will be times, on the search to feel God, when you are a co-pilot on someone else's understanding of living a life connected to the Highest Divine Energy (God). You are learning the ways of the path. You are being gifted the opportunity to witness the beauty of traveling through the eyes, experiences, understandings, awakenings, and guidance of others through the books, the classes, the talks, the earth angels, and other beings of light who have been Spirit-picked to help you open so that you begin to see life in a new way. They are sent in response to your asking, the invitation you have extended from the sincere desire of your heart, for help. It's nice to enjoy the route of another, being around and learning from those who have forged their own similar path, basking in the scenery of the way they traveled to God.

But they are not meant to walk for us.

The time when it's just you and the Divine Connection will surely come. It may seem that this part comes abruptly, out of nowhere, but often we ignore the warnings that a transition is upon us, and we hold on longer to the comfort of where we are. We can handle this stage of the journey. Even if it is scary and we aren't ready, deep down we know it is time to go at it alone. No more running, it's time to be free from the things you are running from. In this alone time, your heart can unburden in full admission—safely: "Yes, this hurt me." "Yes, I hurt them."

Let any regret, any heartache, any guilt that has been waiting for an exit; let it all come up. No more pretending. This is the time to be transparent in complete freedom. The heart becomes self-cleansing because you have given it permission to purge the things that do not allow it to open. So let the tears come, creating rivers of release.

Remorse flowers forgiveness, compassion, and openness. It is necessary for the journey and the connection to flow.

I let it all come up, not because I am so courageous or without fear, but because I know these dark nights are what my soul needs to be free. These hard moments have a purpose. They are preparing me to meet the part of me that I thought I would never walk in. So, I sit, and I allow, each day, to bring to the doorway of my heart what is ready to be seen, acknowledged, and released so that I can meet myself in a new way. The point of meeting me in this new way is so that I can receive and understand who I have always been, who God always is, and the connection that we always have.

The alone time is what we often avoid because there is a level of honesty with ourselves, about ourselves, that is necessary. This level of honesty is revelatory but can be piercing and challenging. You learn about your blind spots when opening up your connection, and how you react when the road veers into spaces that are emotionally tough. You see different things when you are navigating through your internal atmosphere, and you must be honest about what you see.

The alone time is essential to clearing the connection points of the heart, to keeping them clean so Divine Flow is not intermittent. The time alone is the beginning of our training, our development in Truth.

There comes a time when you have to be alone so you can hear how God sounds to you. You need time to learn how to discern between your voice and the Creator's, and it's in this time alone that this is honed. It is a time for you to come face-to-face with you.

12:52pm / How I grew Today

ON GOD (PART 1)

I'm sitting and wrestling with my feelings about God. It's one of those days where my faith is not the strongest, my doubts are. I no longer want this back-and-forth, in-and-out relationship with God. What's really behind these doubts? "Tell me all the things you have thought about me and who you think I am," I heard so clearly in my spirit, so with full trust, without fear of judgment, I said, "OK."

I knew You through my grandmother's eyes, heart, and tears that would come as she prayed and paced, creating trails of praise and worship all over the house.

I knew You through the sudden "Thank You, Thank You" that I would hear as she gave You gratitude for waking her up that morning and starting her on her way, or as she cleaned house, hers and others; ran errands; cooked; and even when she fished; anytime, really. It didn't take much for her to show You how grateful she was. I knew You were important to her, and she would always tell me how important I am to You. Her tears confused me. I thought You made her sad. Later I would find out that they were mixed, tears of joy, peace, gratefulness, most of the time. My grandmother always talked about how You were coming back soon. "Get ready," she would say. That is what she believed, and that is what she imprinted upon my heart. All I could imagine was the earth shaking and people crying, begging to be saved. The Rapture.

I was afraid of YOU.

This was probably my most impressionable memory of seeing someone in a relationship and interacting with You when I was younger. Conversations about Your wrath and Your punishment overshadowed the ones about Your love.

I did not understand You, but I wanted to.

There was this anxiety that formed for me around You, intertwined with the feeling of being judged. That thing about the world ending and getting ready for it created so much fear in me, and a hyper-awareness of my flaws and my mistakes. There was so much misunderstanding about who You are, and what I wasn't, and it stayed with me for a long, long time, building these crazy wide and dense walls between us. One was stamped with "You have to be perfect" and another with "Prove your worthiness before entering." Getting ready meant becoming perfect, to gain love and access to You. I mean, I was used to doing this in my day-to-day with people, but with You too? Those walls hid the truth about Your compassion, forgiveness, acceptance, and the reality of my oneness with You.

The thought of You made my head spin and my heart run for cover.

You always felt secondhand to me, passed down; I didn't think I could ever feel You firsthand. I thought I needed a go-between, an intermediary, to reach You. I wanted to know you for myself, but I did not think I could.

Just like going to college, you were not optional in my house. I have so much gratitude for this foundation, but everything always felt rote and rehearsed, never fresh and flowing. I felt at a deficit.

Over the years I gained a ton of knowledge about You, but it lay dormant without a real understanding of how to apply it, or how to break through my confusion on how to draw closer to You.

There was a part of You I had yet to touch. I thought maybe that was supposed to be reserved for when I got older. Older came, and I was still confused. I continued believing because that was what I was told to always do. My head was in. My heart was not.

It was the hardest thing for me not to see You as the God of my youth, this hybrid, human/wizard/Genie-like caricature that is hard, almost impossible, to please. Vengeful, a God full of rules and not interested in hearing what I have to say.

I have had so many questions about what it means to be in Your presence. I don't know how many people I've asked about their experiences with You. I didn't trust that I knew how and if I would know what to look for when You showed up. I didn't realize You were already here, and I just had to open up. From where I sat, being one with You seemed impossible.

You were complicated to me, and my wounds made You even more complicated. I treated You like I treated many of my relationships here on Earth, in my daily life: guarded, distrusting, never showing You all of me.

But I did talk to You. Well, I didn't realize that I was talking to You. I just thought I was talking to myself on those days when I thought I had no one, having a real one-to-one with myself, unburdening my heart. I didn't realize that's where You were. In my sincerity, honesty, and in the abandonment of my self-consciousness, I was speaking to You too.

My mom used to tell me, "God's voice is still and small." So I listened for You. I paid attention and tried to find You by following many different paths to encounter and connect. There were so many detours and traps. One day, I stopped, and I asked You, "Who are You? What do You sound like? What does being in Your presence feel like? How can I hear from You? Have I heard from You already, not realizing it's You?" I tried to attune my physical ears to hear You, but it was my heart and my soul that needed attuning.

12:56pm / How I grew Today

DEACTIVATE THE CHIPS

We have these chips in our minds and in our hearts. Wounds, informing our everyday lives. Some call them old tapes that play in the background. I call them chips. They are embedded, some very active and easy to trigger and some that are embedded and not as active but are still there as reminders. In order to deactivate these chips, we first have to be aware of them and see what they are trying to show us. Remember, on the other side of the chip is who we really are.

My chips: lack, scarcity, feeling inferior and beneath everyone, having no voice, feeling unseen and unheard.

What have these chips shown me? That I am worthy, I am abundant, I'm equal to all. That my voice is important, and it is beautiful, and I have to hear and acknowledge my voice for myself, even if no one else does. That I must see and honor myself, see myself as God sees me, even if no one else does. The chips must be challenged.

Our connection to Divine Energy will flow to us our true identity and deactivate the chips.

A MOMENT TO FEEL

What are your chips, and what are they trying to show you?

6:03am / How I Grew Today

JUST PASSING BY

When I was disconnected from my heart, it was very easy for me to be influenced by the hearts of others, taking on their beliefs without seeking deeply within myself to find what I truly believed.

And when it came to healing, I thought simple awareness, without taking the steps to apply what I was learning to my life, was enough.

I was just passing by, mimicking, walking alongside. Not really making the path my own. The path to live connected to the Highest Divine Energy is not meant to be walked for you. You must walk it yourself, through your life experiences, not just through what you are reading or the things you hear about from others. The understanding is not enough, it must travel from your head to your heart. You have to apply everything you are learning to your own life, daily. The deep work holds beautiful nuances of the journey. It's the awareness, and the application, that deepens the connection. You can travel far or cover as little ground as you like. However far you choose, do it with your heart open. Let love lead the way.

TWO

CONNECTING

The search leads us to the place where we realize that we are directly connected to God. It is now time for our hearts to open to the connection. What flows through that connection is God's love. It is purifying, healing, constant, forgiving, and gracious. That love flows through us and then from us.

We must allow our hearts to be unburdened and cleared of things that inhibit flow so that our connection remains fluid. Some of us must learn how to be kinder to ourselves; others must learn how to feel again, how to be still, or how to allow our hearts to break so that space can be made within, trusting that they will be put back together again. Some may have to learn all these things, and that's a beautiful thing. The connection to Divine Love produces a heart that is encouraged and willing to grow in compassion for oneself and others, the ones who want to connect, repel darkness, and are delighted by the light of love; the intention of every waking moment is to live from this place. An open heart that is connected is present and understands that there will be many moments to awaken to deeper love.

I DON'T HAVE THE RIGHT . . .

I don't have the right to speak to myself in a negative way.

I have no right to punish my heart and ignore my hurt in the way that I do.

I do not have the right to mistreat myself.

I don't have the right to dismiss, compare, criticize, and be so hard on myself.

I have no right to put myself down, to punish my heart with so much self-doubt, to feel unworthy and undeserving.

I have no right to be unkind, to withhold love, or to betray myself. Anything outside of love I have no right to inflict on myself.

I have no right to disparage my name and create thorns of shame, fear, guilt, and anxiety that cause so much suffering.

What am I saying to the Creator?

What are my words and thoughts saying to the Light that went into the creation of my soul?

If I BELIEVE I am made in the image of God, who I BELIEVE is love and beauty, kind and compassionate, I don't have the right to treat myself as if I don't carry that same spiritual DNA.

A MOMENT TO FEEL

What have you been saying to yourself? In what ways have you treated yourself badly? Make a list of those things that you have been saying to yourself and the ways you have been treating your-self that have not been kind, then dis-card them; rip them up, burn them, flush them. Make another list, fill it with good things (I had to do this over the course of some days because, honestly, the good didn't come to mind as easily as the bad), and place it somewhere that you love—in your favorite bag, in your favorite spot in the house—or spray a fragrance on your list that makes you happy when you smell it. Do something that draws you to it in a positive way. Read it as often as you can.

GIVE IT BACK . . .
(THE DARK STUFF)

That energy that isn't yours
That hurt that isn't yours

That pain inflicted upon you that isn't yours

That rude comment that has nothing to do with you

Give it back . . .

That misunderstanding you've been replaying
over and over in your head

That mistake you keep seeing yourself through

Give it back . . .

That gossip
That offense
That hopelessness
That defensiveness

That jealousy
That untruth
That lie
That shame
That guilt
That anger

Give it back . . .

That rejection
That slight
That betrayal
That dismissal
That unworthiness
That feeling of inferiority
That doubt

Give the energy back to where it came from.

A MOMENT TO FEEL

When you realize that you have been buried under things that are not yours, free yourself. Return to sender, STAT. Whose stuff do you need to put in a box and allow them to hold from now on? Whose anger have you been holding? Whose insecurities have you been carrying so long that they have become a part of you and how you see yourself? You can give it back now.

And the beauty of it all is that they don't even need to know you are giving it back because it isn't about them anyway. It is about you being responsible for yourself; for your energy, your peace, your ability to forgive and to love.

1:11pm / How I grew Today

QUESTIONS AND ANSWERS

Q: What kind of things have buried your connection or have been in the way of you trying to connect?

A: I've been thinking about that. I remember when I was like eight, I had a fight with my sister, and normally I would have just sat there and taken it, thinking I deserved it. But this one time, I decided to fight back, and I can't remember if I bit her or hit her. But seeing how my anger and willingness to retaliate made her feel, I saw and felt a side of me that I didn't like. I didn't like how I felt and how I made her feel, and I said to myself, "I don't want to make people feel bad. I don't like that feeling." So here lies the beginning of my hiding and pretending, because I wasn't sure how to stand up for myself and be heard in a healthy way. I wasn't discussing these feelings with anyone, and from the things I saw my mother experience, being punished for speaking up for herself, unable to fully use her voice, I thought some people can speak up and others can't. I was trying to figure all of this out in my own way. So I came up with my own solution, and that was to always hide my true feelings. Good or bad. I just went along. You do this long enough, you start to lose your sense of self. Your voice weakens until it's barely audible, and then you start to take on the voice of others, or voices that will be pleasing to others. This goes on until you are so used to being anything other than you that being yourself disappears as an option. You begin to feel constricted, smothered, by everyone else's needs and wants. This is a natural progression that starts by denying who you are. What you thought was a good thing by getting along and going along became the very thing that stood in the way of truly yourself and, ultimately, your ability to truly love others deeply. Not being authentic buries the connection and spreads damage all around. It affects your worth, your confidence, and the way you see yourself. I never felt good about how I looked. I had a terrible relationship with food that affected my self-image. I didn't think I was smart. I questioned everything about me. I was indecisive and lacked confidence. I lacked trust in myself and was constantly anxious, full of so many doubts and fears. I gave up authority and thought I had to trust others because I couldn't rely on myself.

Another thing that buried my connection was thinking I didn't matter. I felt insignificant, but at the same time, I felt included and good to be around because I was amenable. I didn't have the courage to disagree or add my opinion into the equation. I was too concerned about how other people would respond or feel if I spoke out about anything. I felt like a fraud. I betrayed myself a lot, and I held a lot of shame for that and anger for not being strong enough to be me.

So yeah, these are some of the things that covered, diminished in my sight, my right and my ability to connect. Not giving myself the grace to grow and accept all of me, not accepting the grace God has given me, and looking outside of myself for validation, significance, and worth.

6:06am / How I Grew Today

KEEP GOING

I rolled around on the floor last night, saying, "It's too hard, I can't do this. This is too much. I'm tired! I want to stop!" Knowing I will not. What I am doing is necessary so my soul can align with my spirit. Where would the stop lead me? I have seen enough now to make me not want to turn back, but it is hard, and I feel like I have to say it is hard, to get the feeling away from me. It can be challenging, when something new is revealed and you see it (awakening), and you have to let go of the old even when you know the old no longer serves you. It's hard to love when you can list endless reasons not to love. It's hard to forgive someone when they are still full of anger and resentment toward you, and you can feel it. It's hard to do the right thing and not take the easy route. When the easy route is waving to you so cheerfully to come on. It's hard to walk away when you are used to staying. It's hard to see all your stuff and love yourself when you can't see why you should. It's hard to feel all your hurts and heal them; the pain of the soul can be sharp. But keep going.

Keep Going. Don't Stop. Keep Going. Don't Stop.

Those hard days are hard. But they will pass. For real, they will. You must walk them. Walk them slowly; take your time. But walk through them.

I was always in a hurry, wanting to have the answers and to no longer be triggered by all my stuff, and I wanted clarity, yesterday. And the lessons, I was over them. My impatience and resistance to just relaxing and letting things unfold caused me a lot of uncomfortable moments. I was tired, spiritually fatigued. I didn't want the hard days to come, but they had to. Those days had to happen. I needed to understand, on those hard days, what was still wounded in me that made things so hard. I needed those days.

Let them come. Keep Going. Don't Stop.

BE EASY

Be gentle with yourself while traveling this road to feel God. You are feeling yourself in ways you never have before. Your opening heart is delicate and tender during this time. It is waking up, coming alive in a fresh way, rousing the sleeping, stagnant places. They have been sleeping for some time. Places you used to go, you may not want to go anymore; you are becoming more sensitive to the energies around you. The energy of people, places, and things that used to be familiar and bring comfort may not have the same effect anymore. All the opening and waking can be alarming. But be easy.

This is the time when you are learning how to listen, how to sense what is around you and how to give your heart what it needs.

A MOMENT TO FEEL

Allow yourself to feel all that is happening in you, without judgment. You can do it; I promise you can. A new version of you is coming into being. Give yourself permission to change.

7:11am / How I grew Today

OUTTAKE FROM AN
AWAKENING MOMENT #1

When you have a moment of awakening, sometimes you're like, "Man, I can't believe I used to think the way I did," or "I can't believe that I treated someone the way I did." You want to run and tell everyone you ever hurt that you are sorry, including yourself.

It feels so good.

2:37pm / How I grew Today

MOVE TO LOVE

Truly loving is not always easy. If it were, then everyone would be lining up to love their neighbors as themselves—it can be hard to love your neighbor and yourself at times.

But move toward it. Move toward love in your heart. Feel it. Feel the vibration of it; the energy of it. Feel the reality of it. It is real.

You may hear people say, "Use your heart." Like a battle cry. But what does that mean to those of us who have yet to be brave enough to use it, to trust it? And what about those of us who don't have the slightest idea how to do either?

On the way to your heart, you will find the reasons why it's been so hard for you to use your heart.

You must be willing to meet yourself in honesty. You must be willing to be OK with everything about yourself; the hard stuff should not push you away but, instead, bring you closer. Open your heart and live from there.

Know what your heart feels like when it is closed and when you have allowed it to open. This awareness is so important.

A closed heart has to be cleansed of all the things that are keeping it closed in order for it to open and allow love to flow. When the heart is closed, it can harden from the congestion of untruths. Fear, worry, anger, distrust, anxiety—these things make it almost impossible to feel the flow of Divine Energy trying to get to you, sending you the courage to open up.

The heart is meant to be open and to be shared. Receiving the flow lets us know that we are in alignment with the highest part of ourselves, engaging and living from the Spirit of creation.

Our point of connection to Divine Energy is the heart. If it is cloudy with hurt and dusty with pain, we will not receive a clear connection, and what we experience in life will be seen and felt through that pain, colored by the dust. How do we keep the connection clear? By being honest with our hearts, true to ourselves. This is what is necessary. Every slight or betrayal, every time we go against what we know we should do, it will add more dust to our connection, blocking the flow.

The heart is where we feel, where God lives in us and where we nurture, grow, and communicate with the Supernatural Intelligence of His Light.

It needs our care. The condition of our hearts determines the condition of our lives. We can no longer ignore it, hurt it, abandon it, belittle it, dismiss it, or second-guess it. It is where Spirit speaks to us, guides us, reveals things to us, corrects us, gives us insight, and loves on us.

Our heart is primed, and God is there waiting.

When we realize love can never be depleted, that's when we will experience the fullness of what the heart is able to teach us, to supply for us. Through every experience, things will no longer be splintered into good or bad. It will be all good. Live from here.

When our heart is open, we allow truth to lead.

And when we speak to others from this place that is led by truth, love, care, and kindness, God is there.

6:33pm / How I grew Today

SOME THINGS
I HAVE LEARNED
ABOUT LOVE

+ I remember not being able to tell myself "I love you" without feeling this cringe in my gut, almost of embarrassment, as if it were shameful to say. As if it wasn't okay for me to feel that way or say those words to myself. I also could feel how much I didn't mean it when I said it. So, for a long time, I stopped saying "I love you" altogether. Our first love should be ourselves. We should make it our mission to love ourselves so much.

+ When we love from the parts of us that have yet to be healed, we love in a way that is limited. Those parts of us need to be healed. The love I have for myself plays a role in the way I love others and the way I am open to God's love for me. Unconditional self-love isn't selfish. It is a necessity. If I only love myself under conditions, I'm going to create conditions for loving others, and I will continue seeing God's love as conditional.

+ Love is God's greatest gift to us. We were created from Love to love. Love is our essence. It always has been and will be.

+ There are some who find it hard to believe that God loves them. I have been there. I know what this feels like. Walking the path back to my heart has been the key to understanding how untrue that belief was.

+ Loving myself bridges the gap between God and me. It closes any separation that I may be holding and fills it up with oneness. I can only let in and give love as much as my heart is open to receiving and giving. The journey to my heart increased my understanding of the love that the Creator has for me. Love is the heart and language of God. I shake my head when I think about how much I misunderstood the gift of Divine Love given to all of us. And then I give thanks for being awakened to the understanding of how sweet, gracious, giving, and complete this Love is. We don't have to search for love in another, with hopes we can find some for ourselves. We already are LOVE.

+ I used to think of love, romantic or familial, as transactional, never unconditional, and I only thought about it from how I was receiving it and never how I was giving it, which was also transactional and conditional. This is what I thought real love was.

+ Love does not require anything in return for it to be real. It just is. Love is life's greatest energy. As I'm writing this, I realize that deep down, I never thought anyone really wanted my love. What kind of energy have I been projecting?

+ Love is about putting love into action, being present, using our hearts, showing care, embracing, and connecting with each other.

+ We are always inside of an opportunity that can move us to a place of truth and deep love if we can see it that way, if we can separate the experience (good or bad) from its purpose to bring us to greater love.

+ Love knows everything is as it should be. If we are open, love will always lead us to more love. Even the things in my life that have been hard have shown me how to love from a deeper place, expanding for me what love means, and the many ways that are offered that become a greater expression of love.

+ The paths we travel to love can vary. I have traveled to love through fear, facing some scary and difficult situations. Even though I was afraid, the courage to keep going eventually led me to find love and appreciation for my deep strength. I have traveled to love through sadness, experiencing loss and heartbreak (both non-romantic and romantic) that I thought I would never bounce back from, only to find it had expanded my heart. On the other side of sadness, I gained an immeasurable appreciation for life and an expanded capacity to love. After the tears and the lessons, love renewed me, and I saw the beauty of being able and willing to love so deeply that nothing can take it away.

+ And love itself has been a road. Loving my son from the depths of my soul has shown me how unconditional love and acceptance for another, expecting nothing in return, is possible and beautiful.

+ Being authentically you, in love, is your greatest opportunity to serve God. Why? Because you are expanding His light by your ability to recognize and hold His light in you.

+ The biggest realization I have had about love is that my love is not dependent on someone else's love for me. I am responsible for being love, and giving love, even in the face of something or someone unloving. This revelation and my continued ability to grow in this has changed my life.

+ It is a privilege to love. Love is the reward. Just think about how good you feel when you love and expect nothing in return. You have no fear of your heart being broken, because you realize that it could never break. Your heart is filled with love.

+ Forgiving, believing, caring, goodness, kindness, peace, light, God . . . all these words mean LOVE. Guilt, shame, resentment, competition, comparison, and jealousy all keep us away from love.

+ A quiet and peaceful mind is love.

+ Love is not exclusive; it is all-inclusive. It includes everybody.

+ Jesus was here to show us how to love. He is the perfect example to show us what pure love is. I want to always live by His example. I want to see all the places I am not so I can love more fully.

+ Love shows all sides. Light and darkness. It allows you to see more than just the offense of a person or situation. It frees you up so that everything is illuminated in the light. This makes us stronger, wiser, and more discerning as our love deepens. And eventually, everything we encounter will be met with love.

+ Love offers no mistakes. Love is light, and light offers us healing, shows us the purity of a thing, and gives us direction and correction when we need it. Love clears the way for us, removing anything in the way of love, giving us more occasions to show up in love.

DIRECTLY CONNECTED

I am,

we all are,

directly connected. To what?

To Divine Love.

To God.

To the love that requires nothing more than for me to be aware of my worthiness of love, knowing that if I understand this fully, everything else will align.

My relationship has been umbilical to this connection (God) and will always remain that way, gently tethered and supplying me. Is there known evidence of its being? One, I have witnessed a new morning. Two, I am able to breathe deeply. And three, my heart provides me with the sweetest beat of life force, flowing through me as I move my body and give thanks for the day. These are miracles that we all witness daily.

When we begin to see our connection to everyone and everything, that is when life changes, and we realize the true meaning of "We are never alone." We start to see that we all have the connection point, the outlet, within us, and that we all are worthy of this relationship; it isn't just for a select few. It isn't this exclusive club only for some and not for others.

We all have open access to the creative power of the Divine if we choose to plug in and become one with the Source that supplies us with love.

Your reverence and appreciation for all things, seen and unseen, grows. Every experience, every situation, every person, every perceived failure, every rejection, has all been playing its part, bringing its contribution to your doorstep so that you can begin living fully as you were meant to live—as the real you. This is why who we are and what we do matters to more than just ourselves. As you stand in all that you are, in full love, you allow those who you connect with to do the same.

There is no separation between us and the connection.

We do not have to rely on our own strength. The beauty of the connection is that it never goes away. It is anchored.

Even when we become stronger in our connection, we may revert back to our old ways of kinking the flow to our hearts. We will experience times when we feel unplugged. There will still be things lurking in the crevices of our hearts that we need to cut the power to so that we don't allow them to pull us away, to unplug us.

What I now understand is that I am the one who kicks myself in and out of feeling the flow; plugged, unplugged. I am the one who determines whether I live in connection or outside of it.

What are my signals that I have disconnected and plugged into a source of things that do nothing to raise my energy? Worry, guilt, shame, doubt, anger, envy, jealousy, unworthiness. Being critical, judgmental, defensive, deceitful, or fearful. Anything that does not make me or someone else feel loved.

I am the one that can choose, in challenging moments, what to give my attention and energy to. And even in that choice, if I am unable to choose the Source that will elevate me, I am given an opportunity to see where growth, understanding, and love are still needed.

So now I am aware of how this works, and of what I do not want to experience life through—disconnection from my heart followed by feeling separateness. I am aware of what I feel like in and out of the connection. Out, I am afraid. I feel lost, ungrounded, sometimes I feel stuck and unsure of myself. In, I am free. I let go and I trust. It is my choice. And I know I must choose day by day, and on tougher days, minute by minute, to stay connected.

ON GOD (PART 2),
A LETTER OF LOVE

I remember the night I began to understand my relationship with You in a different way. I had a moment of awakening on my balcony. This time there were no mud pies with cereal. It didn't happen when I was playing and happy; it happened when I was in a space of spiritual doubt, and I was frustrated. My heart was heavy, and for the first time, I realized what being brought to the point of surrender felt like. I didn't want to give up, but I wanted to let go. I wanted to let go of all the effort and trying and getting in the way of the flow. I was aware of myself being in the way, and I was ready to let go and mature to the level of trusting You, not needing to understand the mechanics of things. I wanted my faith to be bigger. I sat outside and stared at the stars. Then my gaze moved to the trees and the river below me. For some reason, I paid really close attention to everything I was seeing, just taking it all in, and after a while, I said, "God created all of this, everything I'm seeing right now, these trees, this body of water, the sky, and the universe. It's so vast and amazing," and then it was like a curtain had been opened, revealing what had once been concealed from me. You were waiting for me to get to this point of letting go. My spiritual eyes opened more.

You revealed so subtly my connection to everything—people, animals, energy, the trees, the universe, the oceans (I mean, there are 33,000 species of fish and 200 billion galaxies)—and I felt connected to it all. Such beauty, such intelligence, and it hit me hard. I am part of this creation. Why did I think that creation did not include me? I had this immense understanding of all my misunderstandings that I held as truth. I had not realized how ostracizing my own thoughts were about my connection to life, to You, and I know how this sounds. But I'm being 100% honest about how I felt and the things I believed. I had been living life with these thoughts of exclusion, at the ground level of everything I believed about You and me. I thought You were separate from me, and in that moment on my balcony, I awakened to our oneness. It was in the letting go that I came closer.

I feel free. Freer than I ever have in my life. I now know that I live inside of Your Love, Your Creation, too.

I allowed my heart to open and freed our relationship from the box that confined us to rules.

You have shown me that through trust, belief, faith, and love, I can move the mountains in my life, mountains of fear, doubt, unworthiness, shame, guilt, and more.

You are not a human figure, wielding Your staff of judgment. You are far beyond anything I have reduced You down to, seeing at the level of my limited natural vision.

Your Spirit moves through me like waves; each ripple reveals something different each time. My human mind tries to see if I can identify a pattern, but I can't.

The things I need to know of You are constantly unfolding and being revealed, at the right pace, as You have designed for it to be, for me.

You have touched my heart and brought it back to life. That fire that is You that was once small has grown bigger, and greater. I see my connection to Your Spirit, and although I still have questions, more about me than You, I know undoubtedly that I am connected and one with You. I see that I'm the plug (my heart). You are the outlet, and Your Spirit is the energy that flows through the connection.

Creation is love and You are the Creator. The Creator of all things.

When I create, I am close to You. Whenever I am writing, cooking, loving, forgiving, dancing, singing, being understanding, being there for a loved one or a friend, in all these things, I am creating love. And You are right there.

When I am worried, depressed, anxious, fearful, doubtful, jealous, complaining, blaming, comparing, these things move me away from inspiration and creation. They destroy and tear down the fabric of love that I have been weaving in my heart, creating things that are not in Your image. And there You remain, my constant, graciously waiting for me to return to You.

I have the freedom to explore Your nature, to understand for myself who You are. You never tire of my many questions. You welcome them. You are always present. Right here, right now. Your presence is felt when I see a beautiful work of art or hear a beautiful melody that brings me to tears. I also feel You in the things in life that have been unpleasant, making the beautiful out of the ugliness that life has offered me.

You know every dot that needs connecting and every part of me that needs to be touched. You are a master weaver, artist, musician, architect, astronomer, teacher, parent, and friend.

You give me the right things to say at the right time, my thoughts that are of love and that bring life to me, my words that hold the energy of love that speaks life to others. You are the one who puts people on my mind and heart to call or to whisper a prayer of healing or gratitude for.

You are my intuition and my revelations. You are.

When we live plugged in, hearts open, with love, there is only one source of pure energy that we are tapped into. And that is You. I've seen the evidence of this countless times, when I have conversations with different people, at different times, within the same week or day even, and those conversations are all aligned with the same message of love or healing. I also see evidence of this when those I know, who are also connecting and on their own path to living deeply in Your light, have the same things come up in their lives, the same themes being dealt with during the week. This synchronization is an alignment with Your Energy, Your Spirit.

You have changed my heart. There is no longer an undercurrent of fear when I speak of You, only love. You are understanding, gracious, patient, forgiving, accepting, and caring.

God is light, and in him is no darkness at all. 1 John 1:5

Every good gift and every perfect gift is from above. James 1:17

I understand this now. Your light is love, and love is perfect. It is freeing, cleansing, forgiving, and compassionate. It does not judge, it doesn't punish, it doesn't reject, it doesn't withhold. It isn't transactional. It is corrective, gently illuminating and redirecting my path where needed, only for love's sake.

You co-create with me, so my energy matters. I must be in alignment with joy, peace, and love to bring about beautiful creations that are of the highest vibration.

When the wind kisses my face on a cool autumn day, You are there. When the rain pours, clearing and making way for the new, You are right there.

I see how You are in everything, the homeless man on the corner, the preacher in the pulpit, the poet that has been inspired. I feel You in my questions, prompting me to go deeper. I feel You when my doubts take hold, and You encourage me to believe. I feel You in my moments of sadness, placing joy and hope in my heart, delighting me in simple things, reminding me that You walk with me.

You changed the way that I speak to myself because I now know that I am also speaking to You, and You showed me how to pour love into my heart so that it flows from me. (Thank You.)

Through Your patience and compassion, You uncovered mine. (I am grateful.)

Jesus walked this earth as the full expression of Divine Light and Love. You embodied Him.

There are beings of light who have committed their lives to serve others by spreading light, goodness, and kindness; they have been awakened by that love. I, too, have been awakened and claim my alignment to Your ways.

Your understanding has given me the courage to be honest with You. My faith, my beliefs, and above all, my trust have deepened. Your Divine inspiration and love I now feel so deeply.

Your Spirit lives in me, and that makes me want to live free, just like You created me to be.

I love You with my whole heart. Thank You, God.

6:44pm / How I grew Today

IN THE MOMENT OF
BEING PRESENT

Being present is how we connect with ourselves. We can perceive our hearts, minds, bodies clearly when we are present. It is where we get to know ourselves deeply, it's where we start to understand the language of our heart, how we speak to ourselves. There is so much offered to us in the present.

When I am present, I don't miss the guidance, the messages, the wonders all around. When I'm thinking about something that happened 10 years, 10 hours, 10 minutes, or 10 seconds ago, I am in the past, and I miss the guidance, the messages, the wonders all around.

When I am present, I am where God is.

5:55am / How I Grew Today

OUTTAKE FROM AN
AWAKENING MOMENT #2

You have to remember; this is where you are on your journey. This is where you are on your path to love. This is where you are in the process of awakening. And "he" is where he's supposed to be, "she" is where she's supposed to be, and "they" are where they need to be. We can be on similar levels, yet still different levels. The levels don't matter. The main thing is that we are walking through it. Treat everyone with love and you'll be good. Love is the great equalizer in every part of the journey.

11:11pm / How I grew Today

IN THE SPACE BETWEEN MY THOUGHTS IS WHERE GOD IS

In that stillness, that is where flow is. That is where my heart is open. That is where creation takes place. That is where possibility and choice reside. In the letting go and in feeling, allowing yourself to be enveloped by freedom without flinching in fear of being so free. That fear has been because of me doubting that I can trust freedom to remain, doubting that it can be this effortless in the letting go, and doubting that I can live free even while things around me are still bound. Even while things still happen that can unsettle me, now I believe and know that I have Divine backing and stand firmly in the expansiveness of that space between my thoughts. Worry doesn't reside in that space.

Doubt doesn't either. Only love.

THREE

BEING

We search, decide to awaken, train our hearts to beat the cadence of love, and remember our connection. And now it is time to BE. To fully align with the source of light that created us and that remains within us. Earth is a school where we begin to understand our energy; we begin to connect the dots between what we put out in the world and what we get back. We are here to understand how to live by our spirit, how to be good stewards and master our energy. We start seeing what helps us connect and the things we do that block our connection from flowing, learning to release ourselves from vibrations that are lower so that we can live life from our higher selves connected to higher dimensions. We are here to bring the light within us out of hiding and then use it to encourage and illuminate love on this planet. We let go so our lives can be further transformed. We learn to pay attention and live from the present, in God's presence.

Being is living life awakened, aware, and connected—trusting; silencing the doubts, worries, and fears; and seeing all the guidance that is right at hand, deeply trusting our connection to God.

How I grew Today

EARTH IS A SCHOOL

We enter the earth in tears. Is it because we do not want to be lulled into sleep, uncertain if we will awaken again, or if we will remember how to? The veil is beginning to descend, and we are quickly forgetting who we are: spiritual beings who are one with God. Our memory of where we have been fades. Will we find our way back to that place of wholeness in this new world? Will we remember that we are not alone, and we will never be, as we navigate our way here on Earth, even if it feels like it? This is the place, the school where we are to grow consciously. The training will move us through courses like:

+ The Time of Redesigning

+ Notes on Observing: A Second Set of Eyes

+ Some Things to Learn and Remember about Issues

How I grew Today

THE TIME OF REDESIGNING

Will you allow your energy to transform, to unlearn what darkness taught you and learn what living in light is so that you live life by the largest part of you? Not by your flesh and bones, not by your fears and the limitations they produce, but by your spirit and its gifts? Will you experience living in the kingdom of your heart, in the atmosphere of God's energy, while you are here physically on Earth? Will you be changed and rearranged voluntarily? It's not for the faint of heart. It is not easy. There is no timeframe that will be forced on you. There are no shortcuts. But the reward is great and beautiful; the only question is: Will you allow yourself to be redesigned?

Will you endure the changes and learn to let go and trust the unfolding so that your life can breathe, so that you, who have been encased in plaster and paint, existing underneath façades and the many years of veneers that have kept you bound and lifeless, can be chiseled away? You will be stripped to the studs in certain areas of your life. But if this is what it takes to be renewed, will you stand in the way or stand in faith?

There will be fixtures and other things that you may want to keep but that need to be retooled and rewired because, in their current state, they will no longer work within the new foundation being laid. Old thoughts and ways of being will need to convert so that they operate better in this new design. Your trust will get a complete overhaul, as this is what makes our foundation sturdy so that we live in harmony, balance, and peace. The gaps created by feeling separate from the Original Architect (God) will be filled by your ability to now receive the love, kindness, gentleness, joy, peace, and confidence that you have always been so worthy of.

You will feel different, and that could be startling, especially if you think this redesigning means you have to become a version of yourself that leaves no trace of who you have been. But that will never be the case. The beauty of allowing yourself to be redesigned is that remembering how you used to look helps you see yourself, all the versions of you, and love all even deeper. This process of redesigning leads you to greater compassion and understanding for yourself and others. Everything has the potential to be repurposed and used again more efficiently.

You may feel pulled back and forth for a while, but this is part of the redesigning process, making sure things settle into place.

There may be times when you feel like no progress is being made; that's when deep things are being done. Things at the bedrock of your soul are being restored.

You will be shown aspects of yourself that you may not want to see. Anything that does not align with the new creation—situations, people, thoughts, actions, the way you speak to yourself, how you see yourself, anything that does not bring life—has to be seen (awareness) and removed (released). This can seem like it takes a long time. Hold on.

You will shift continuously, be turned over and over, so that you become free of judgment, criticism, and anything hurtful to your spirit or that does not produce growth in your soul.

BEING

The process may get lonely, and you may feel awkward because everything feels different, but this time is what produces honesty and authenticity. Honesty and authenticity anchor you. You are finally allowing yourself to evolve into who you are truly meant to be. Who you have always been.

Little by little, you will gladly welcome the shifts that happen during the times of being redesigned, however fast or slow they come, because now you see the Divine pattern that takes place when things need a redo or need to be revisited. You embrace the awareness that a change is needed, the releasing, and then the rebuilding. You will always be given opportunities not to become spiritually complacent while here on Earth. Take them. The times of redesigning are, and will always be, so that you remain free. So you remember that the Creator, and His Creation that is you, are one. Breathe this in.

How I grew Today

NOTES ON OBSERVING:
A SECOND SET OF EYES

Some bird-watchers love watching birds because the intentionality of watching (merely looking at the birds' external characteristics), seeing (gaining deeper insight into how they think by observing their movements), listening (to how they communicate), and hearing (discerning the communication) connects them to nature, bringing life alive in a new way by watching it lived out through other life-forms.

I spent the day quietly watching, seeing, listening, hearing. I spent the day letting my energy lead.

Seeing what it liked and disliked.

Listening to what it responded to automatically.

And hearing what took it in a new direction—what increased it and what depleted it. Like the watcher of birds, I watched myself.

I took notes; I wanted to see, feel, and hear what I allow to disconnect me from the Source that gives me life and plugs me into what drains and siphons life from me:

An unwanted phone call, an unexpected change or disruption in my daily routine.

A disgruntled neighbor, negative thoughts that come at me left and right, never-ending, it seems. Our energy is magnetic, and we determine what we bring to us and all the things we see.

I watched and I saw how easily I allowed the lower rungs of energy to hook me. I just handed my vibration over so easily and let the lower frequency have its way. It didn't need much to grab me, just a thread to latch on to, spiraling me down to the floor. Suddenly, I was swimming in place because of the weight of it all, stuck in the same space for who knows how long. I didn't protect myself. I didn't think I would ever find my way up again from that low place. A single hook, one thought, one thing, dragged me down to another level where all the accumulated worries, anger, doubts, and fears had been lingering, looking for a place to land. Now they had one. They tag-teamed old beliefs, thoughts, and things that happened years ago. I was drowning in a sea of negativity. Even things that would normally lift my energy merged and became depths of negativity. Doubt had poured in. And all I could see before me were all the reasons why I should not trust, not love, why I should be agitated and remain hopeless. And all the energy-raising, high-vibration-giving things that I knew to do, I told myself they were not worth doing. I did not believe. All the things that were dark performed and knew I was watching.

And in a flash, I started to see what was happening. I witnessed as they turned into monsters. I saw how I fed the negativity by giving it so much energy and made it grow. There was no one there who did that except me. I was creating and directing this movie that was playing out in front of me. And since I was the creator of my own distress, I could redirect it.

I could get up. I didn't have to give in and allow the darkness that came in the form of my thoughts, perceptions, and old triggers to keep me in submission, robbing me of peace, disconnecting me from light. I didn't have to listen to the things that drained my life force and capped it off. I didn't have to go low.

Even though it was hard and felt almost impossible to believe I could do it, I started feeding myself as much light as I could consume and digest, broth-like statements at first, until I could really affirm the bold truths. So a simple "No, these things are not true and are irrelevant" was all I could muster, but that was enough to starve my spirit of the negativity.

By arresting the thoughts and my reactions, my belief started to grow again, and when belief grows, trust blossoms. And the movie changes.

A MOMENT TO FEEL
(MOVIE MAKER)

What movie are you making? A nightmare, a drama, one full of sadness? Look. And see. See if you can find some good and create a movie that reflects that, and watch your connection get stronger.

How I grew Today

SOME THINGS TO LEARN AND REMEMBER ABOUT ISSUES

+ Issues, tests, problems, and trials will come.

+ Some big. Some small. It's the world we live in here on Earth.

+ Issues play a part in our learning. Our tests offer us opportunities or experiences to learn through.

+ Challenges birth new ideas. Some of my greatest moments of inspiration and revelation were preceded by an issue.

+ Issues hold purpose. Often, we don't see what this purpose is until we are on the other side of the problem.

+ Issues give us the experiences we need to awaken and the opportunity to release us from the things that do not serve us (feelings of unworthiness and inadequacy, insecurities, lack of confidence, distrust, fears, doubts) so that we can live as the complete, pure, positive beings we already are. Issues can appear in areas where we still have some work and expanding to do.

+ We are not immune to them.

+ We can't pray them away. And as crazy as this may sound, we shouldn't want to pray them away. They fortify us, make us strong.

+ We should not spend time trying to figure out how to control the issues (which is exhausting, I know, because I thought I could).

+ Issues that stem from unaddressed wounds become problems, bubbling up to get your attention. Like old invoices that you forgot to settle, they resurface for payment, and never at the best time.

+ Issues emerge not to punish or shame you, but ultimately to release you of their debt, even if it feels shameful or is painful.

+ Don't allow issues to shake you, frighten you, threaten you to your core. Imagine them as clouds, or as trees passing as you drive. Can you hold that cloud in its place in the sky? Can you keep a tree in your eye view as you drive by? No. So let them pass the same. There is always a solution. Stay calm so you can hear and notice the solutions when they come. Don't ignore them. And at the same time, do not dwell on them. When you dwell on them and get your energy entangled with issues and problems, the bigger they become.

+ Treat them as guides, leading and protecting you on the way to Light. Let them show you what needs to be seen. Life has many different facets. Issues are one. And just because you have chosen to walk on the path of living in connection to God does not mean you will be exempt from hard things happening. It is not about living a life without problems; it is about learning how to respond in a new way. How to overcome difficulties with new insight, with more reliance and trust in yourself and God.

MEDITATION

PSALM 91
FOR
PROTECTION. COMFORT. PEACE.

Morning. Night. And whenever I'm feeling disconnected, stuck, worried, doubtful, fearful, or just a bit out of sorts.

How I grew Today

THE BATTLE FOR YOUR CONNECTION (YOUR LIGHT VS. DARKNESS)

There is a battle for our connection.

Remember, even though we can't see it, the battle is always raging. There is a war waging, all the time, vying for our light.

This battle has taken place on various fields for me—my heart, my thoughts, my beliefs, and my perception. It has been waged in the fabric of my relationships, the way I have loved, in my communications, and in the relationship that I have with myself.

When you feel you have your footing, darkness will come after your peace, your joy, your light, your trust, your desire to understand, your assignment, your will that is free. Darkness wants you to choose it as a source.

You tell yourself that you know the many ways of darkness and you will keep your light, but it can be tricky and blindside you. The more you connect to Light, the stronger darkness can become. Stay connected. Your connection is your refuge.

Understanding this is important. Remember, just because we choose to walk the light path doesn't mean we will be free of problems or ambushes from dark energy. We just become better equipped in handling them when they appear.

The attacks of darkness can be blatant or surprising. But you will know when you have been infiltrated. Darkness will always lead you back to sadness; doubt; feelings of dread, melancholy, worry, or fear; anything that is not of Light.

Our artillery, when used with belief and trust, keeps the opposing energy on its side. Darkness will still try, but if you stand firm, darkness will flee.

The battle will test you, to see how deeply you trust Light. The game darkness plays is to trip you up with discouragement and doubt, accusations and criticism. It will push you to see if you will continue to choose Light; if you will continue to trust, believe, and choose love. This battle will use all that it knows of you to connect you to the side that is not Light. It works to bring your energy over to darkness.

Darkness will pull out all the stops, reminding you of your past, taunting you with things you are working to heal, or have healed, just to see if it can stop you, make you turn around and do nothing to save your heart.

Darkness is misleading. It can look flashy, exciting, and alluring, making us think that its ways are the best ways—"Get a lot for doing a little," "Take the easy way out," or "It's okay, no one is watching, no one will know." Remember that you have chosen a position, and the rules of engagement for the side of Light are different. You are moving through life with the intention of honesty, integrity, and trustworthiness. Darkness will try to entice us to get us so invested in its antics. If we get swept up by its deception, we will certainly crash hard. When we are disconnected and in so much pain, regret, guilt, or shame, we forget that Light surrounds and protects us and is there waiting for us. Instead of wrestling on the side of darkness, going tit for tat, remember the strength of our arsenal, which comes with heavy artillery and the highest connection.

Darkness runs on tracks that are parallel to Light. The paths are so close, and it doesn't take a huge leap to cross that line either way.

We are engaged in this war whether we are conscious of it or not. We are either actively protecting our connection so we remain connected no matter what is going on in our lives, or we are allowing our connection to be taken and plugged into a source that will flow to us fear, limitations, worry, guilt, doubt, anxiety, sadness, everything that is not of love.

Note to Self: On those days when you feel like you are fighting, remember that Love loves you and always will.

We may slip and fall and find ourselves on the track of darkness and make what we think are mistakes, but really, these are opportunities for us to see where we are and what we need to regain our position on the track of Light. Perfection is not the objective, love is.

Our fight is strong when we don't doubt. We will have moments where we doubt, but face those moments with the intention of not staying there.

Know which side you are fighting for.

ARTILLERY OF LIGHT

Love

Compassion

Patience

Forgiveness

Emotional stability

Confidence

Courage

Breathing

Self-control

Your quiet time

Prayer

Stillness

Meditation

Your conversations with your heart

Honesty

Joy

Understanding

The willingness to know Truth

Kindness

Realizing your wholeness

Authenticity

Always being encouraged to live
from your highest self

Always encouraging others to do the same,
no matter if that benefits you or not

Understanding you are a part of this
Energy that is so pure and holds no darkness,
and rooting your confidence there

Trust

Faith

Belief

Calmness

Unity

Acceptance

Inclusion

Encouragement

Caring

Helping others

Anything that produces healing and love

ARTILLERY OF DARKNESS

Anger

Jealousy

Comparison

Chaos

Ego

Distractions

Lies

Negative thoughts

Unbelief

Doubt, worry, and fear (big weapons that
are used by the dark to destroy)

Unworthiness

Gossip

Complaining

Judging

Defensiveness

Being easily offended

Dishonesty

Discord

Discontent

Doubt

Division

Disbelief

Exclusion

Reminding you of your shortcomings
and encouraging you to take
the way that is easiest

Frustration

Insensitivity

Lies

Greed

Being hurtful

Those thoughts that creep in that say,
"You can't do that, you don't and won't
ever have what it takes"

Those worries about your future
(they are not loving, they are not light)

Revenge

Negative self-talk

Anything that takes away from healing and
that does not produce love

I F

If my energy is up or has fallen so low to the ground.

If my faith and my ability to believe have been weakened by something that has happened or has not yet happened.

If I am disappointed and discouraged.

These things disconnect me from my heart and weaken my connection. He is always there. These are the Ifs that affect whether I am able to feel Him.

A MOMENT TO FEEL

Have you ever noticed that when you feel low, or down about something, it's hard to pray or meditate? I have found that these are the most important times to pray and meditate.

Take one day and write down every time you feel your energy shift from high to low. Write down what caused the shift: what were you thinking, where were you, who were you around, what time of day was it? When you feel low, it's hard to feel God. Become aware of the things in your life that create the feeling of separation from God's love in you.

OBSERVATION . . .

We are interconnected with everything.

A MOMENT TO FEEL

Have you ever considered your connection to the universe, the ocean, nature,
all living things? Take a moment to reflect on your relationship to creation.

THE BREATH

Close your eyes. Open your heart.

Breathe in for 4. Hold 7. Out 8.

Repeat 4 times (more if you need more time to relax). Go weightless. Return to your normal breathing.

Shed your skin, your bones, your organs, everything. Don't attach to anything.

Now, imagine yourself as light radiating all the way through.

Sit with this and breathe.

Now, as your silhouette of light, hover above the space where you are sitting, float up to the ceiling of the room, and with each breath move higher.

Roof (Take a breath)

Sky (Breathe)

Beyond the sky (Breathe)

When you are beyond the sky, just hover there; allow yourself, as light, to blend into all that is there, all that is around you, and just let go.

Breathe. Rest.

How I grew Today

THE EVOLUTION OF MY PRAYERS

My prayers have evolved. So has my life. They used to be anguished, anxious, fearful, and distrusting. So was my life.

I now pray affirmingly instead of desperately. Instead of "Please give me clarity" or "Please give me inspiration," my prayer is "Thank You for clarity" or "Thank You for inspiration." Praying this way comes from a foundation that affirms my ability and right to choose from the many possibilities that are rooted in truth and love. It aligns my heart with what I really am.

Guidance comes quickly and at the right time when I pray with deep feeling, and even deeper faith, with my heart wide open, and without the undercurrent of fear or rejection, trusting that my energy is aligned divinely, to an answer that is always perfect to my prayers.

I am never NOT in prayer. Those inner questions directed to my heart are my prayers. Those conversations that I have with myself in the wee hours of the morning or when I'm in the shower, driving; whenever my heart is open and honest and feeling every word I speak, those are my times of prayer too.

It emanates from me through my actions, my thoughts, through what I believe, my words, and my energy.

I make sure to look at what I have been praying and affirming over my life not only through my words but through these things also. These things must be aligned and in sync.

My whole life is prayer, my beating heart, my breath, the blood flowing through me, and every moment is a moment to give thanks, to ask affirmatively, and to be in alignment with the Creator.

A MOMENT TO FEEL

Think about this.

Where do your prayers originate? Are
they coming from doubt and disbelief,
or a place that affirms your Divine alignment? Are you praying from love? Or are
you praying from lack? Are your actions,
thoughts, beliefs, words, and feelings all
aligned with God's creative energy?

How I grew Today

(A N O T E T O R E M E M B E R)

SOME MORE THOUGHTS
ON BEING PRESENT

In the present moment . . . that's where inspiration and creativity are. Give full attention to what's in your hands to do right now . . . in this moment. And watch the answers and the guidance come . . . in the moment of being present.

How I grew Today

I was gifted with a vision that appeared in the form of a dream. It was such a gift because it held so many messages for me. They keep unfolding.

It was one of those dreams that remained with me for a long time. You know those you can't shake, and you remember every detail? Those dreams that feel so real that you think they really happened? It was one of those. It was so visceral.

THE WOMAN WHO APPEARED IN MY DREAM (THE DREAM THAT KEEPS ON GIVING)

She felt familiar to me. I thought maybe I met her in passing on the street, at a restaurant, or maybe I saw her at an airport.

She was beautiful. She looked golden. Like the sun had given birth to her.

She was confident and graceful; she moved like she was attached to invisible strings. She seemed to float or glide, not getting hung up or caught on anything around her.

She was healed. Unclothed, naked of limitations, concerns, regrets, guilt, shame, fear, and doubt. She was free. She knew who she was, and she knew that her very existence was a gift that warranted gratitude to her Creator. You could feel her devotion to living life fully and truly. She walked tethered only to truth and love.

Her spirit was refined. Her scars were now evident only by her calm, composed, and loving nature. A refinement that only answering the call to search can produce.

I shadowed her, making sure she didn't see me. She was so sure of herself and mindful of everything she did. It was her whole being that I longed for every day. To be that free and comfortable with who I am.

She was powerful in a way that exuded ease, and it was effortless. The total opposite of what I thought power looked like. She was gentle and kind, strong. As I followed her up to these big wooden gates, they immediately opened for her. The Sun lit a communal table where everyone from all walks of life had gathered. The world was represented at this table. I couldn't make out faces, I could only feel the energy and see it moving.

I took my eyes off her for one second, and when I looked back, she was serving everyone from a basket. The raucous and rowdy, the ones who were shy and afraid to reach in and take their portion, all different ages, races, nationalities, religions, and genders. She served the ones that complained, the ones that seemed angry, even the ones that didn't acknowledge her yet took from her basket.

She gave to all, and they all wanted some. They were hungry for it. There was love in her basket.

She was unphased by the variety and complexities of the table. Her presence was still. Her peace was certain. Her joy was ever-present. She served from a deep place. As I observed how she served, she changed the way I understood serving others. It took nothing away from her to be kind, to give, to embrace everyone as they were. It took nothing away from her. And as she served, she seemed to grow. She got bigger; her light got brighter. And I wanted to be closer. Her presence lit something up inside of me, as it did to all who were around her. She got brighter, and we did too.

I noticed that there were others who voluntarily joined in to help her serve. Like a magnet, her light drew them in.

They joined in the flow of love streaming from her. Like me, I imagined they wanted to understand what that was, how they could be that too.

After she served, she went to the top of the mountain where the Sun was about to set. As if to say thank you, it kissed her in gratitude as it was descending for the day. That was the gift she received for her gracious service.

The Sun's favor replenished her and recharged her strength through the power of its light. Her spirit was in an exchange with the light of the Sun, and she got brighter yet again. This abundant energy fortified her with more clarity, so she could see more possibilities, more things for her to choose from in life. The Sun's love refreshed and nurtured her spirit. Her heart was full; all her needs were met through love and serving others.

I had the courage to get closer. With her eyes still looking toward the Sun, she said, "Follow me." She knew I was there the whole time. She led me to a pool of water where a baby with the most beautiful golden skin, like hers, was being baptized. It frightened me at first because it seemed the baby was being held under the water for way too long. But every time the beautiful little girl went under, she would come up for air, taking a trusting breath, unafraid.

Up.

Deep breath.

Under.

Up.

Deep breath.

And under again.

Each time, she too got brighter, stronger, and was replenished. The Golden Woman pointed to the baby and said, "She's you, being cleansed of all the things that are keeping you from loving and accepting the masterpiece that is you. You are being washed of the things that diminish your light and prevent you from seeing the light in others. I am also you. You are being prepared to serve light too. You will offer love to everyone, free of all the reasons the world may tell you to withhold it. You will give light. There will be some who are ready to receive it, and some who need more time, but let that be of no concern to you.

"You will not be alone. There are angels, divine beings of light, right along with God, guiding you. I will be guiding you too. Be patient with yourself."

This vision was my answered prayer. A few days before I had the dream, I was driving down the street, and with all the feeling in me, and with my heart wide open, I said, "I want to be free to be me. I want to walk in who I am, in love, guided by Spirit, graciously, honestly, and lovingly.

"And I want to give love like that too. I want to stand for something so deep inside of me that I do not waiver, ever."

Later, I began to understand what I had been gifted with, and the significance of this dream. It showed me my transformation, my purpose, before I started to walk intentionally toward connecting to God.

All the sifting, shifting, purging, and many moments of awakening have been for the purpose of bringing this vision to fruition, helping me emerge into the me who appeared in my dream. I am walking this path to realize the vision for my life that began to take shape before I was a thought in my mother's mind.

On days when life gets hard and the world I see with my natural eyes makes me weary and beckons me to stop walking, I remember this dream and the point of it all.

This walk is to strengthen and develop my whole being so that I can live and serve graciously, honestly, and lovingly, just as I asked.

BE. GRATEFUL.

When you feel stuck, be grateful. When you feel unsure, be grateful. When you are happy, be grateful.

In your abundance, be grateful. When problems appear, be grateful.

When you can be a blessing to others, be grateful.

Things big and small, it doesn't matter. Just be grateful. Every time you want to complain, be grateful.

Every time you are upset or feel low, look for something to be grateful for in that experience. Train yourself to move through the uncomfortable and look for the gratitude. Even if it's thank you for that breath or my beating heart, or for not being triggered by things from the past, or for being triggered, showing me what still needs my attention and healing.

When I keep saying "Thank You, thank You, God, for blessing me," it is my mantra, my prayer, that keeps me in Divine alignment, giving me more things to be grateful for. Abundant things for which to say thank you.

Soon, you will begin to see how miraculous your gratefulness is.

BEING

A MOMENT TO FEEL

Gratitude has become more than a list; it has been an energy shifter for me at times. It has changed my heart on many occasions when I thought I could not find anything to be grateful for. Taking the time to pause and be grateful helped me find the good in simple things during the hardest of times. Sometimes just me saying "Thank You" without a list of things was all I could do, and that was more than enough. Make a list or just say thank you, especially when it's hard to find something to be thankful for.

BE. IN JOY.

Where joy is, you will do well. You will allow and love and give. When you are joyous, you will stay open. Be in joy.

A MOMENT TO FEEL

Joy is a magnet that draws more joy to you. What brings you joy? I'll go first: my son and cooking.

CALLING ALL LIGHTWORKERS

It's time to step fully into your calling.

It is time to fully integrate into your task and champion light in everything you do and direct it to everyone you meet. Of course, not by force, by example, by living in Light. Then those ready to blaze their own path will come easily. It's up to them, not you. Remember that.

Shine, encourage, inspire, and always be honest (apply these things to you first). Take care of yourself. Share with others what that looks like for you.

Pray.

Meditate.

Ask questions to the Divine.

Heal.

Forgive.

Be happy. Be in joy.
Be grateful. These are so
important to your light.

Have compassion.

Be unafraid to be you; all the stuff
that brought you to the point of
searching is in the past now.

Keep your energy up. Notice the
things that cover you in darkness
and negativity. Notice when you
are not enveloped in love. If not
vigilant over your own energy, you
can unintentionally be used by
darkness to diminish light. Impart
light in the world; your teaching,
your helping, however you are in
service to others. Make sure to
keep your connection clear.

It is difficult to support and
be in flow if your own heart
is burdened and you feel
low. When our connection is
weakened by dusty cables,
it's difficult to get a clear
signal from God for guidance.
When this happens, take
some quiet time, be still, pray,
meditate, ask the questions
of your heart and listen for
the answers. You want to
flow life from the Source of
all creation.

Remember, you have walked
the path and worked diligently
and intentionally to get to
this place of authenticity. This
is a great reward; bask in your
newly discovered gifts.

Trust   Trust   Trust

This whole walk has been
about learning how to trust
God and yourself, which you
now know are one.

Be light. Be the example. Be strong in your decision to live a life of light, both feet in. Remember, we are all Lightworkers if we choose to be.

And don't forget that we have healed and connected so that we can share and spread the light that has come ablaze in our souls, to increase the strength and number of light warriors on this earth who are living to feel God.

How I grew Today

THE MORE

You are here now. Living in the space that was calling you. More found you. And you are finding more, every day. More love, more peace, lighter.

You now understand how to navigate through the forces that we can't see that may tempt you to backtrack and step away from the connection. You now are aware of how to stay connected.

You realize that the search for more has been about learning to be authentic, certain about your connection and how the connection works in your life. Your trust is going to grow deeper, and you work to keep your connection strong. You trust yourself. Doesn't it feel good? Can you believe this is you? You trust yourself because you trust the Connect, God. You realize that your ability to learn how to trust yourself was so key.

You are using your heart, and when you use your heart with love, you know that you are being led by the Spirit and can trust the flow. You now believe that you are one with God.

Because of the strength of your trust, you may notice that the messages, signals, and guidance are flowing easily and consistently—as they always have, you were just sleeping and unaware of your guidance. No more second-guessing. You are awake and will continue to awaken to things deeper. You see beyond words, hurts, and misunderstandings.

You understand that more is not a destination. It's a knowing and assurance, a new way to approach life.

More is living life from your spiritual being, nurturing your inner self. More is also realizing that when you feel good about yourself and walk in your connection, you will see more good in you and in the world around you.

How I grew Today

FLOW

And that same voice inside that whispered, "There's more," is now telling you that it is time to flow. Go with it.

Out of what seems like nowhere, grace has stepped in and swept out the last part of the way you used to think and your limited understanding, and you let it leave. You let go.

You have been honest with yourself. You gave up the pain, the losses (what you thought were losses), and the unhealed things in your heart so that you could expand.

Your grasp was tight, and that kept you far too small and confined. You would never have allowed yourself to be renewed and expanded in the beauty of God's presence, with teeth and fist clenched, holding on to things that would never produce life.

You listened and let go.

The issues that came up, the obstacles you faced, you learned how to breathe through, calm yourself in their wake, and release so you did not get so worked up when things happened. Things stopped making you so nervous and scared.

Those relationships that needed to change or go, the time that you needed alone with just you and God, the purging, the things you had to face about yourself that only you could face:

The redesigning
All the forgiveness that had to be done
The hurt that had to be seen and attended to
Why the way you spoke and loved yourself had to be corrected

Now you see the reason for it all; you are a vessel for fresh living water to flow through. All of this has helped bring you here. You are in Divine alignment.

You have stopped kinking your connection to the flow of the Spirit with doubt, fear, and distrust. You gave God the space needed to settle and inhabit your heart so that you could receive His Spirit, which has embedded in it all the guidance and intelligence you need.

Now you know so deeply that you are the receiver; your heart receives the messages sent from God. You are tuned in to the right station. You are present, paying attention, and trusting what you see.

You see the brilliance in the way everything is connected, and that everything can be used as a gift of guidance, giving you instructions on where to go, what to do, and how to respond. You have gotten out of the way and are allowing the energy to flow through you.

When you get out of the way, you start living like the things in nature, trusting God's timing and ability to unfold life perfectly. The right times to sow, nurture, grow, shed, harvest; the right time to stay the course or change directions. You understand that storms come to cleanse as do the unexpected things that happen in our lives.

Like nature accepts what life offers—it has no choice but to—and flows with the rhythm it was born into, so do you. You have stopped resisting what is naturally unfolding for you.

Being disconnected from flow feels so unnatural to you now.

"Am I connected?" or "Do I know how to connect?" are no longer questions. You have matured to the place where you know you are connected, and now, part of your Divine assignment is to stay in flow.

Now, your heart is leading, and you are living through trust. You no longer need to know every detail, the how, the when, the why; you just flow.

BEING

GIVE IT BACK . . .
(THE LIGHT STUFF)

That love
That peace
That joy
That forgiveness
That encouragement
That freedom
That trust
That belief
That faith
That good word
That good deed that happened right when you needed it
That moment when someone took the time
to stop what they were doing and listen

Give it back . . .

That nonjudgmental ear
That understanding
That new perspective

Give it back . . .

That story about how you went through something
That testimony about how you overcame something
That honesty
That realness
That authenticity

Give it back . . .

A MOMENT TO FEEL

Seeing where I can be light in the world is very important to me. It has helped deepen my connection, and now I have more reverence for all things around me. Where can you give more light back to the world in your day today?

LIVING IN TRUST

We SEARCH because we are being called.

We CONNECT when we answer.

When we decide to live by our spirits, we show up in the fullness of who God called us to BE: free, real, authentically living as our higher selves.

God is not complicated. Humans complicate God. Once trust has been mined from deep within, we become vessels for Divine power to flow through, for God's light to shine, and from this higher dimension, we begin to walk in the power and authority that is our right so that we can inhabit all the gifts available to us.

We all have God's outlet in us. There is not one person who does not have the ability to access God. Not one. No matter how bad or undeserving we think someone is, even if that someone is ourselves, there is still the ability to plug in to God's love and feel His presence at any time in a person's life. And it requires nothing but an open and willing heart and the desire to plug in. Connect to the other end of your love, no matter how tattered, tired, or imperfect you think you are. Give everything to it and receive everything you need. I intentionally walk in the love given to me. And I share that love with others. I am not perfect—some days are harder than others—but I do my best to be loving, kind, and helpful. That is always my intention; it is my heart's way.

Today, be kinder, sweeter, and gentler with yourself. Today, feel a little more than you did yesterday, and trust, trust, trust as much as you can. And tomorrow, trust a little more.

ABOUT THE AUTHOR

Marquita L. Moore is a writer, author, and inspirational conversationalist. Her personal healing journey inspires her work.

Marquita spent over 10 years of her professional life in the entertainment industry, working in marketing and brand management. After years of feeling unfulfilled and ignoring the feeling that there was something deeper in life that she was not tapping into every day, she began intentionally walking her path to living authentically, awakened, and growing spiritually.

Marquita is a graduate of Hampton University's School of Journalism and is originally from Birmingham, Alabama. She currently lives in the New York / New Jersey area with her son River, where she spends her time helping heal and feed the souls of others through her How I Grew Today platform.

Learn more at www.howigrewtoday.com

SPACE FOR YOU

You've read my notes and reflections. Now use this space for your own. For those who need a little more guidance, I bulleted some reflection points on each section to start you on your way.

SEARCHING

Reflection Points:

+ If you sit and look back over your life, can you identify moments when you felt or even heard something inside of you say, "There is more to life than this. There is more to life than what I am experiencing or seeing with my naked eye"?

+ Where in your life do you not feel free? Examples: Relationships, work, home life, mind, heart, voice

+ What have you been looking outside yourself for that you haven't been able to find on the inside? Examples: Love, acceptance, worth, validation

+ What are you using as distractions?

....

....

....

....

....

....

....

....

....

....

....

....

....

....

....

....

....

115

| SPACE FOR YOU

....
....
....
....
....
....
....

117

....
....
....
....
....
....
....
....
....
....

....

....

....

....

....

....

....

....

....

....

....

....

....

....

CONNECTING

Reflection Points:

+ What are the things that pull you away from connection? What is in the way? Examples: Are you condemning yourself? Are you holding on to guilt, shame, or anger?

+ What are you carrying that you need to release?

+ Where are you hurting?

+ Reflect on Love.

SPACE FOR YOU

....

....

....

....

....

....

....

....

....

....

....

....

....

....

....

....
....
....
....
....
....
....
....
....
....
....
....
....
....
....
....
....

....

....

....

....

....

....

123

....

....

....

....

....

....

....

....

....

....

....

....

....

....

....

....

....

....

....

....

....

....

....

....

BEING

Reflection Points:

+   What are you observing about yourself?

+   What does walking in Light and by Spirit mean to you?

+   How do you want to live your life?

....

....

....

....

....

....

....

....

....

....

....

....

....

....

....

....

SPACE FOR YOU

....

....

....

....

....

....

....

....

....

....

....

....

....

....

....

....

....

....

....

....

....

....

....

....

....

....

....

....

....

....

....

....

129

SPACE FOR YOU

www.ingramcontent.com/pod-product-compliance
Lightning Source LLC
Chambersburg PA
CBHW020357130626
46549CB00006B/2318